Pedal It!

HOW BICYCLES ARE CHANGING THE WORLD

MICHELLE MULDER

ORCA BOOK PUBLISHERS

Library and Archives Canada Cataloguing in Publication

Mulder, Michelle, 1976-
Pedal it! : how bicycles are changing the world / Michelle Mulder.
(Footprints)

Includes bibliographical references and index.
Issued also in electronic formats.
ISBN 978-1-4598-0219-3

1. Bicycles--Juvenile literature. I. Title. II. Series: Footprints
(Victoria, B.C.)
TL412.M84 2013   j629.227'2   C2012-907692-9

First published in the United States, 2013
Library of Congress Control Number: 2012953464

Summary: Bicycles can be used for many things apart from transportation.

Orca Book Publishers is dedicated to preserving the environment and has printed this book on Forest Stewardship Council® certified paper.

Orca Book Publishers gratefully acknowledges the support for its publishing programs provided by the following agencies: the Government of Canada through the Canada Book Fund and the Canada Council for the Arts, and the Province of British Columbia through the BC Arts Council and the Book Publishing Tax Credit.

Cover photos by Getty Images
Back cover photos (top left to right): Michelle Mulder, Kerri Finlayson, Workcycles/Henry Cutler; bottom left to right: Lon & Queta, Samuel Abbott, Hansenn/Dreamstime.com
Design by Teresa Bubela

ORCA BOOK PUBLISHERS
PO Box 5626, STN. B
Victoria, BC Canada
V8R 6S4

ORCA BOOK PUBLISHERS
PO Box 468
Custer, WA USA
98240-0468

www.orcabook.com
Printed and bound in Canada.

16 15 14 13 • 4 3 2 1

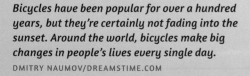

Bicycles have been popular for over a hundred years, but they're certainly not fading into the sunset. Around the world, bicycles make big changes in people's lives every single day.
DMITRY NAUMOV/DREAMSTIME.COM

For Bob and Betty.

Contents

CHAPTER THREE:
ON THE MOVE

CHAPTER FOUR:
PEDALING FOR CHANGE

Introduction

Me, my box-bike and a lovely load of flowers. Box-bikes are one of many kinds of cargo bikes. Cargo bikes are built to transport both people and a surprising variety of loads!
GASTÓN CASTAÑO

What do you like most about riding a bicycle? Is it the freedom of flying down the road with the breeze tickling your skin? Do you notice sights and sounds you might miss if you were in a car? Do you thrill at going far and fast on your very own power?

I love cycling for all these reasons. In fact, I love it so much that I've never owned a car. I pedal to the grocery store, to visit friends, to the library and even to local schools to talk to students about my books. When my daughter was eleven months old, I put a child's seat on my bicycle, and when she got too big for that, I got a special kind of bike called a box-bike. It has a wooden box in front big enough to hold her, her best friend and a few bags of groceries.

I love cycling, and I love traveling too. Wherever I go, I notice bicycles. Sometimes they're common. Sometimes they're not, and sometimes people use them in very surprising ways. Once, in Argentina, I watched a man power a knife sharpener by pedaling a bicycle, and I began thinking about just how much a bicycle can do. This book will take you on a ride around the world, where you'll see bicycles being used in some astounding ways. Grab your helmet, hang on, and have fun!

In Buenos Aires, Argentina, knife sharpeners sound a special whistle as they pedal around a neighborhood. MICHELLE MULDER

On My Route

I was fifteen when I bought my first bicycle, and I rode it for almost twenty years. One summer, I pedaled it more than six thousand kilometers (thirty-seven hundred miles) on a trip across Canada. Eventually, it looked so old that friends suggested I buy a new one. I refused until the gear system broke beyond repair. Finally, I donated the bike to Recyclistas, an organization in Victoria, British Columbia, Canada that gives new life to old bicycle parts. I like to imagine pieces of my old bicycle riding around Victoria and maybe even retracing my steps across the country.

The first bike I bought, resting here at Lake Magog, Quebec. MICHELLE MULDER

CHAPTER ONE

Who Thought This Up, Anyway?

THE WALKING MACHINE

What's the most important part of a bicycle: the tires, the chain, the pedals or maybe the brakes? Would you believe that early ancestors of the bicycle had *none* of those parts?

Picture a time before airplanes and cars, a time when people walked everywhere unless they had horses to ride. In 1817, the German nobleman Baron von Drais got tired of walking and invented a "walking machine" to help him get across his gardens faster: two in-line wooden wheels, connected to a wooden frame, with a handle connected to the front wheel for steering. The rider of the "Draisienne" would swing a leg over the frame, push back with alternate feet and roll forward. Riders could go up to eight or nine miles per hour. Walking pace is about three miles per hour. This increase in speed was exciting to many Europeans, and the Draisienne became a popular fad among those who could afford one.

THE BONESHAKER

Unfortunately for Baron von Drais, all roads in those days were dirt, gravel or cobblestone, and his new invention didn't work very well on bumpy surfaces. Eventually, people lost interest in the walking machine.

An engraving of a Draisienne from the early 1800s. Photos from those times are hard to come by because the camera was only just being invented. BRIDGEMAN ART LIBRARY

Cycling wasn't always the smooth, gliding experience we enjoy today. Imagine going down a bumpy road on this 19th-century bike. They didn't call them "boneshakers" for nothing! PJHPIX/DREAMSTIME.COM

Within a few years, inventors began to experiment with pedals that would turn the wheels. Early versions of pedals were more like levers. In fact, the earliest pedaling systems were actually hand levers that riders used to add speed while running. No one liked the idea of taking their feet off the ground to ride.

It wasn't until the 1860s that inventors created a popular pedal. Some people credit French carriage maker Ernest Michaux for the invention, and other people say it was Pierre Lallement, who worked for him. The pedals and cranks were attached to the axle of the front wheel, and the rider could slow down or stop by pedaling backward.

Everyone wanted to try it. Businesspeople saw an opportunity, and bicycle manufacturing took off. Many large cities built schools to teach people to ride the *velocipede*, which means "fast foot." Riders needed to have good coordination, be very strong and be willing to bounce around a lot. Velocipedes could weigh as much as 68 kilograms (150 pounds)—the weight of an adult!—and riding them was exhausting. Riding on bumpy surfaces was so uncomfortable that these bicycles were often called "boneshakers."

How many differences can you spot between this bicycle and a modern one?
HANSENN/DREAMSTIME.COM

On My Route

Almost two hundred years after the Draisienne was invented, "push bikes" are becoming popular again, but this time it's toddlers who are using them. Bicycles without pedals help small children learn to balance and go fast, even before they have the coordination needed for pedaling. We bought our daughter a push bike when she was two, and now her favorite pastime is soaring along the sidewalk with me running after her!

My daughter and friends gather at a local park for a push-bike rodeo.
MICHELLE MULDER

In 1879, this boy was photographed with his father, E.W. Shipton, who was a member of the Bicycle Touring Club in England.
LORNE SHIELDS COLLECTION

BIKE FACTS: Orville and Wilbur Wright invented the first successful airplane in 1903. They learned about steering, balance and momentum when they were bicycle builders and mechanics, and later they tested their wing designs by riding bicycles that had those wings attached!

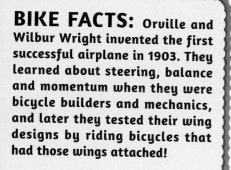

THE HIGH-WHEELER

In 1871, British engineer James Starley began selling the "Ariel," or high-wheeler, a bicycle that was less painful to ride. Made of metal and with solid rubber tires, these bicycles had a huge front wheel, which helped them go farther with each turn of the pedal. Ariels were much more comfortable and efficient to ride than boneshakers, but much harder to get onto. Here's what you had to do.

1. Stand behind the bicycle.
2. Put your left foot onto the step just above the little wheel.
3. Use your right leg to push off along the ground, causing the bicycle to roll.
4. When you get enough momentum, straighten your left leg, jump forward into the saddle and start pedaling. Oh, and watch out if you are going down a hill, because the pedals go faster and faster as the front wheel spins faster!

These high-wheel bicycles were known as penny-farthings in England because they reminded people of two coins side by side, a small farthing and a large penny. The new high-wheelers were popular with young men, but families had to be rich to afford them. A bicycle cost as much as an average person earned in six months. Women did not ride high-wheelers very often unless they worked for a circus. Women's clothing made riding almost impossible. (Imagine riding a bicycle while wearing rigid, tight underclothes and a skirt down to your ankles!) Also, high-wheelers were dangerous to ride. If a dog or a large rock or any unexpected object got under the front wheel, the rider would go flying off and land on his head. In fact, the expression "taking a header" was invented because of high-wheel bicycles.

THE "SAFETY" BICYCLE

How could a bicycle be efficient and safe at the same time? Cycle makers solved that problem in the 1870s, when they moved the pedals from the front wheel to the bicycle frame and attached them to chain drives. (We'll see how this works in the next chapter.) Now a bicycle with two small wheels could go just as fast as a high-wheeler. This new kind of bicycle was known as the "safety." John Kemp Starley, James Starley's nephew, introduced the first successful chain-driven bicycle in England in 1885, and suddenly the high-wheelers were being called "ordinaries" because they weren't so special anymore.

But while the safeties *were* safer, they were also less comfortable. Riding a safety was much bumpier than riding a high-wheeler. (Remember the boneshaker that also had a small front wheel?) Tires were still made of solid rubber, so wheels had very little cushioning against the rocks and bumps they rolled over. For a while, bicycle riders had to choose between a safe bicycle and a comfortable one. Then a man in Ireland had a great idea.

AIR IN YOUR TIRES

In 1888, John Boyd Dunlop was a veterinarian, an inventor and father of a boy who loved riding a tricycle. The jarring rides gave the boy headaches, though, and Mr. Dunlop was determined to come up with a solution. What if, instead of using solid rubber, the tires were filled with air?

Mr. Dunlop made three air-filled tires and tried them out on his son's tricycle; soon bicycle riding changed forever. At last people could choose bicycles that were both comfortable for their bodies and safe for their heads.

This bicycle's front wheel is even smaller than the back one, which is a big change from the high-wheeler. Other than the size of the wheels, though, bicycles haven't changed much in over a hundred years. LORNE SHIELDS COLLECTION

BIKE FACTS: In the 1890s, some doctors warned that bicycling was unhealthy. They said it could cause Bicycle Eye (tired eyes), Bicycle Face (tight face muscles), Bicycle Hands (from gripping too hard) and Bicycle Heart (from the strain of going uphill)!

This woman was one of the early bicycle riders in Ottawa in 1898. Imagine trying to ride a bike with such a long skirt. She might also have been wearing a corset—a rigid "cage" she pulled tight around her to make her waist look smaller. Luckily, as more women began riding bicycles, fashion began to change. LIBRARY AND ARCHIVES CANADA, PA-132274

When a woman in Victoria, British Columbia, dared to wear bloomers in public, it made the news as far away as Brooklyn, New York.
BROOKLYN EAGLE, MARCH 25, 1895.
COURTESY OF THE BROOKLYN PUBLIC LIBRARY

ON YOUR BIKES!

With all these new changes, bicycles became more and more popular in Europe and North America. Upper-class families rode bicycles around parks or on Sunday outings, and owning a bicycle became a sign of prosperity.

As time passed, manufacturers worked hard to make bicycles less expensive. People began to use bicycles as a fast, inexpensive way to get around. Women especially liked the new bicycle designs. They were safer and easier to ride, and the chain and mudguards kept women's skirts reasonably clean. In fact, bicycles became so popular that women's fashion began to change. Shorter skirts and bloomers (balloony shorts worn under dresses) went from being scandalous in the early 1890s to being popular fifteen years later. By the mid-twentieth century,

North American and European women were wearing trousers, just like men. Some people believe that bicycles have done more for women's rights than any other object in history.

Children liked bicycles too, but most families couldn't afford them as toys. Some kids used them for work, though. (Back then, many children worked to help their families. This is still true in many countries today.) Boys as young as ten worked as messengers. Each day they put on uniforms and went to the local telegraph office. There, a man used a special machine called a telegraph to send messages to and receive messages from other telegraph offices. Whenever a message arrived, the operator printed it out and gave it to a bicycle messenger, along with an address. The messenger pedaled the message to its destination. In those days, this was the fastest, most modern way to send someone a message.

Fifteen-year-old Wilbur H. Woodward, Western Union messenger number 236. The photo was taken in 1912 by photographer Lewis Hine, whose photographs of child laborers helped encourage governments to make strict rules against children working when they could be in school. RECORDS OF THE US HOUSE OF REPRESENTATIVES, NATIONAL ARCHIVES

These boys worked for the Canadian Pacific Railway as messenger boys in 1924. It was a busy job that required a lot of pedaling, and messengers were usually paid for each delivery, not for how many hours they worked. GLENBOW ARCHIVES, ND-3-2322

A boy on his way to school in 1899.
GLENBOW ARCHIVES, NA-1899-6

Father and children with their bicycle.
LIBRARY OF CONGRESS, LC-DIG-npcc-04408

BIKES FOR MORE KIDS

Did you know that many of the people who invented cars started out as bicycle mechanics? Henry Ford, for example, used much of what he knew about bikes to build his first automobiles.

When cars first appeared on the roads in the early twentieth century, they were expensive and exciting. Not only were they faster than bicycles, but the drivers never had to worry about their legs getting tired. As more people bought cars, fewer adults rode bicycles.

More and more children began to ride, though. Basic bicycle design hasn't changed in one hundred years, but there have been many interesting trends in bicycle styles. In the 1930s, manufacturers added big front lights and shiny parts to make bicycles look like motorcycles. In the 1950s, kids' bikes looked sleeker, like jet planes. And they must have felt about as heavy as a jet plane too. Some of the bicycles weighed about 29 kilograms (65 pounds)—almost as much as their riders!

Bicycles can now be found around the world, and in many countries they're the most common form of transportation. They're cheaper than cars, and lots of people depend on them to get to work, go to school and even to power things like laptops and water filters.

One of the best things about bicycles is how simple they are. And simple technology can make a huge difference to people around the world. But how does it all work?

BIKE FACTS: In the 1960s, toy stores sold battery-powered toys that looked and sounded like motorcycle engines. The idea was to clamp the "motor" between the pedals of a bicycle. With a turn of a key, the bicycle could now roar like a motorbike while the child pedaled down the street!

As automobiles gained popularity, bicycles became cheaper, and more kids got them. Many of those kids dreamed of owning a car someday. These kids have turned their bicycles into something similar to automobiles, just for fun. LORNE SHIELDS COLLECTION

On My Route

These days, a child can ride on an adult's bicycle in many ways: in a seat near the handlebars, at the back or in a trailer behind or even on the side. I liked having my daughter up front, because I could watch her excitement about everything she saw. And people got excited when they spotted us, too! Almost every time we rode together, someone stopped to ask about the seat. And even when we weren't with our bike, passersby recognized us as "that cycling family." Does cycling build a sense of community? You bet!

My daughter enjoys a front-seat view on our bike rides.
GASTÓN CASTAÑO

CHAPTER TWO

How Did We Get Here From There?

W hat do you think of when you hear the word "machine"? Most people think of something with an engine. But bicycles are machines too. A machine is any device with moving parts that work together to perform a task, and when you ride a bicycle, you become a crucial part of the machine. You—the rider—are its engine!

CHAINWHEELS, FREEWHEELS, WHEEEE!

On the old high-wheeler bikes, the pedals were attached directly to the front wheel. Every time the pedals went around once, so did that front wheel. That's why bicycle builders made that front wheel so big: the bigger the wheel, the more distance the rider would cover with every turn of the pedals.

But remember the whole problem of taking a header? For safety's sake, cycle makers wanted to build bicycles that could be just as efficient with two same-size wheels. The secret was to add a few metal discs with teeth (sprockets) and a chain that goes around both sprockets.

Together, the chain and the sprockets are called a "chain drive." Here's how it works.

BIKE FACTS:
A bicycle is made up of over a thousand individual parts. Half of those parts are found in the chain itself.

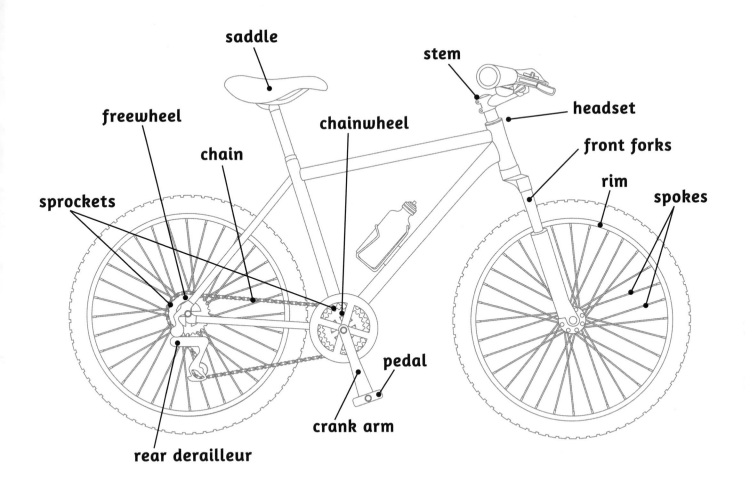

saddle

stem

freewheel

headset

chainwheel

front forks

chain

rim

sprockets

spokes

pedal

crank arm

rear derailleur

A typical road bicycle has about 1,275 parts, so we'll only show a few here!

1. You push down on one pedal.
2. The movement of the pedal turns the chainwheel (the bigger sprocket), which pulls on the chain.
3. The movement of the chain pulls on the freewheel (the mechanism on the rear wheel that allows the wheel to rotate while the pedals are stationary).
4. Because the freewheel is attached to the back wheel, each time the freewheel makes a full rotation so does the back wheel. Because the freewheel is so small, both it and the back wheel of the bicycle go around many times each time you push down on the pedal.

These days, most bicycles have more than one "speed." By pressing a shifter on the handlebars, the cyclist can move something called a *derailleur*, which moves the chain to a bigger or smaller freewheel. When you shift to a smaller one, pedaling is more difficult, but you get more speed. A bigger freewheel lets you pedal more easily, but your back wheel doesn't go around as fast. Easier (but slower) pedaling is good for going uphill or against the wind.

WHAT TOOK YOU SO LONG?

Why didn't inventors come up with the chain drive right away instead of messing around with enormous front wheels for bicycles?

Well, for one thing, people didn't know enough about metal. Many parts for simple machines were made out of iron, which is strong but heavy and difficult to turn into tiny chain links. Other metals were either too expensive or too weak. But then, in the second half of the 1800s, people in Europe and North America invented ways to mix cheap metals to create strong, compact metal parts for machines. Then they built enough machines to fill whole factories. The people who worked in these factories used the machines to make things that had always been made by hand—including parts for simple machines like bicycles.

This new trend of people working in factories instead of making things by hand was called the Industrial Revolution. Without it, we would never have had the strong, compact, relatively cheap parts that people used to invent the chain drive.

LEARNING TO RIDE

Do you remember learning to ride a bicycle? Did it feel like the bicycle had a mind of its own and went all sorts of places

If riding a bicycle is so much like flying, why not put wings on a bicycle? That's what these two fellows did in the early 1900s. GETTY IMAGES

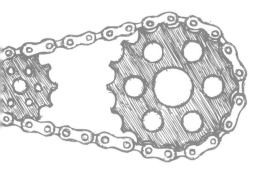

Racing down a hill on a bicycle feels a lot like flying. But did you know that pedaling can actually power an aircraft? In 1979, American aeronautical engineer Paul B. MacCready led a team to develop the Gossamer Albatross, a pedal-powered plane that flew all the way across the English Channel. The 32-kilogram (70-pound) aircraft completed the 42-kilometer (26-mile) flight in 2 hours, 49 minutes. (How's that for incentive to keep pedaling? If you don't, your bicycle-plane will crash into the water below!) NASA

that you didn't want to go? Crashing down to the ground, for example? Learning to ride a bicycle means training your brain to treat the bicycle like another part of your body. You become part of the machine, and the machine becomes part of you.

All that can be tougher than it sounds. Lots of scientific principles are involved in keeping a bicycle upright. In fact, riding a bicycle is a little bit like flying. It's all about balance. Watch a bird fly, and you'll notice that every few seconds it twitches its wings. These tiny adjustments allow the bird to keep its balance in the air and stay aloft. When you ride a bike, your body senses when the bicycle starts to fall over and twitches the handlebars in that direction, which makes the

Designated cycling routes promote cycling and alert drivers of cars to pay special attention to bicycles. WORACHAIY/DREAMSTIME.COM

bicycle lean the other way. This twitching and leaning steadies the bicycle and keeps you upright.

THE BICYCLE REVOLUTION

Once you know how to twitch like a bird and you've strapped on a helmet, you can fly along the road. Riding a bicycle can get you to your destination four times faster than walking would, using only three-fifths the energy. Riding a bicycle is the most efficient way to use human energy to move yourself from one place to another.

No wonder bicycles were big news when they were first invented. Suddenly people without horses could move around faster than ever before. Bicycle organizations asked governments to make smoother roads to ride on. (Later, these new smooth roads were perfect for cars.)

On My Route

When a friend and I cycled from Vancouver, British Columbia, to Saskatoon, Saskatchewan, we collected photos of road signs like this one. The notices were about gas stations, of course, but every time we saw one of these warnings, we checked our own "fuel" too and made sure we got to a grocery store before leaving town. We sure got hungry when we were pedaling over 100 kilometers (62 miles) per day, and food always tasted extra good by the time we sank our teeth into it.

On a long bicycle trip, road signs about "fuel" take on a whole new meaning. MICHELLE BRAZAS

Several bicycle builders and mechanics who loved the idea of speed and efficiency used their knowledge to build cars. Automobiles could go even faster than bicycles, could haul bigger loads and were better for extreme weather conditions. So more and more people wanted cars. No one knew then that cars could harm the environment, or that the fuel might one day run out. People bought cars as soon as they could afford them. Only people who didn't have enough money for a car rode bicycles. The bicycle went from being a symbol of wealth to a symbol of poverty.

Meanwhile, inventors were so excited about how fast cars could go that they forgot about pedal power and focused on combustion engines. But lately, more people are thinking about protecting the environment and their health—and saving money by buying less gas! More and more people are choosing to jump onto their bicycles instead of revving up their cars.

Toronto cyclist James Schwartz encourages cyclists and motorists alike to mount these stickers on their vehicles. Campaigns like this make the roads safer for everyone. JAMES SCHWARTZ

ZOOMING AHEAD

By knowing the advantages and disadvantages of cars and bicycles, we can choose the one that best suits our needs in a given moment. *And* we can protect the environment at the same time.

For short distances, bicycles can't be beat. In urban centers, bicycles help avoid traffic jams and parking crunches. Also, since all vehicles must respect speed limits and traffic lights, cycling in a city can be just as fast as driving, if not faster. In fact, the annual Great New York City Commuter Race has shown that traveling by bicycle is both cheaper and faster than traveling by car or public transportation in that big city. And look how much less space bicycles take up on the road.

Bicycles don't create as much noise and air pollution as cars do. If more people traveled by bicycle for short trips, governments would spend less money on pollution control.

> **BIKE FACTS:** On average, Americans use bicycles for only one of every hundred trips. Using bicycles for two of every hundred trips would save three and a half billion liters (close to one billion gallons) of gas every year!

These photos show the amount of space needed to transport the same number of people by car, bicycle or bus. CITY OF MÜNSTER, PRESS OFFICE

BIKE FACTS: Gasoline fuels cars, and food fuels cyclists. One liter (roughly a quarter of a gallon) of gasoline has enough energy in it for a small car to travel about 65 kilometers (40 miles). With the same amount of food energy, a person on a bicycle can travel up to 1,037 kilometers (644 miles).

They'd spend less on road repair, too, because bicycles are lighter, have thinner tires and don't go as fast as cars, which means they cause less wear and tear on the roads. Also, making space for bicycle parking is less expensive than creating car parking, because bicycles take up far less space.

In Switzerland in 1989, the chemical company Ciba-Geigy was about to build a new parking garage. But first, the company made a deal with its workers: anyone who didn't need a car parking space would get a free bicycle. Two hundred thirty employees chose bicycles instead of parking spots for their cars, so the company didn't have to build a new parkade after all. The bicycles were much cheaper than building a new parking garage, so the company was happy and employees got brand-new bicycles to pedal around on, which put smiles on their faces. What a great deal!

Bicycle parking at Utrecht Station in the Netherlands is compact and well used. Imagine how much space it would take to park this many cars! ZACH VANDERKOOY

BICYCLES MADE FROM PLANTS

Bicycles have great advantages, but they're not perfect. For example, think of all the energy and resources that go into *making* a bicycle. Of course, the materials used to build the average car could make one hundred metal-frame bicycles, but some bicycle builders want to reduce the pollution of bicycle manufacturing even more.

That's why they've turned to bamboo, the fastest-growing woody plant on the planet. Under ideal conditions, bamboo can grow more than a meter (3 feet) each day.

Ghana is a country in Africa where bamboo grows very quickly, and where a lot of people cannot afford bicycles.

This is a "before" picture of a new bicycle frame.
MICHELLE MULDER

Bamboo bikes are sturdy, sustainable and much better for the environment than traditional bicycles. JOHN MUTTER

Yet bicycles can get children to school, get families' goods to market to sell and get sick folks to the doctor. People who are trained in bicycle building and mechanics can earn enough money to help feed their families. In Ghana, as in many countries, bicycles can mean the difference between an empty belly and a full one, or even life and death.

So scientists John Mutter and David Ho founded the Bamboo Bike Project in Ghana to help local factories produce low-cost, high-quality bamboo bikes. These bicycles are very strong and can carry loads of up to 227 kilograms (500 pounds). They also have excellent natural shock absorption, perfect for riding on bumpy roads. This project is good for the environment and good for the people involved.

THE POWER OF PEDALING

These days, bicycles represent not wealth or poverty but good thinking. By using bicycles for what they do best—covering short distances quite quickly, saving the need for parking space and encouraging people to be outside and getting exercise—people have come to see them as an important part of building community, protecting the environment, promoting fitness and reducing stress. Now that we know cycling is good for both the cyclist and the environment, why not use this old, nonpolluting technology when it works best?

Around the world, people are using bicycles in ways we might never have imagined before. The possibilities might surprise you!

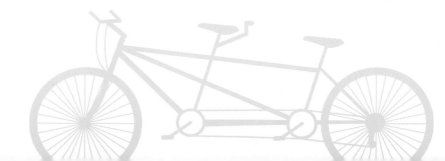

Check out the new bicycles for sale in Hohhot, Inner Mongolia, in northern China. For many people around the world, bicycles are the most affordable and efficient transport possible. NICO SMIT/DREAMSTIME.COM

On My Route

Betty and Bob are dear friends of mine, and anytime I have a question about bicycles, I ask Bob. Cycling has been his favorite mode of transportation for almost seventy years, and his favorite kind of bicycle is a folder, like the two shown at right. Folders are designed to fold up and fit into carrying bags no bigger than a suitcase. He loves being able to pack his bicycle into the car or onto a bus.

My friend Betty poses with the folding bicycles that she and her husband, Bob, rode on holiday in 1977. BOB MCINNES

CHAPTER THREE

On The Move

Ever tried to play soccer on a bicycle? Cycle ball, or radball, was invented in 1893 and is now popular around Europe and in Japan too. The people on each team control the ball with their bicycles or their heads, except when defending a goal. Oh, and usually their bicycles don't have a freewheel (so they can't coast because the pedals are always moving when the bicycle is moving), and they don't have brakes either! MARTIN KUENZLER

Have you considered using your bicycle to carry sixteen of your closest friends, as one rider in a Chinese circus troupe does? Or to play soccer? Or to haul a kayak or surfboard? Bicycles can make fun stuff even more entertaining. (In fact, one Japanese amusement park even has a pedal-powered roller coaster!)

BEYOND FUN

Most North Americans ride bicycles for fun. But all around the world, they're used for hard work too.

Have you ever seen a bike courier zooming a parcel to its destination? Businesses in many cities use pedal power to send local packages and letters. Bicycle couriers are often the fastest way to send something within a city, because they can zip past traffic jams and don't need to spend valuable time finding places to park.

Many businesses choose bicycle transportation because it's better for the environment. Where I live, small gardening companies, organic vegetable delivery services and even a composting service are pedal-powered. The library brings books to public markets by bicycle too.

During the summer months, the Greater Victoria Public Library pedals books to popular public places with the Bike Mobile. Anyone is free to wander by and check out something new to read. I love the idea of celebrating books, bikes and fresh air this way! GREATER VICTORIA PUBLIC LIBRARY

On My Route

Much of Victoria was once covered in orchards, and many apple trees are now on public land. We pedal around looking for bright-red apples, enjoying time with friends in the sunshine and fresh air. When we find a tree, kids play while adults pick, and we carry apples home in bicycle panniers, our box-bike or in a friend's bicycle trailer. Last year we collected—and pedaled home—more than 227 kilograms (500 pounds) of apples for juicing, baking and dehydrating.

Every autumn, we climb onto our bicycles and go apple picking. MICHELLE MULDER

Colby at Share Organics delivers organic fruits and vegetables to homes throughout Victoria, British Columbia. MICHELLE MULDER

In some countries, bicycles become shops on wheels. HELEN COONEY

Businesses on two wheels are especially common in Asia, not only because of pollution concerns. Often, selling from a bicycle is the best business decision. Imagine that you have 14 kilograms (30 pounds) of oranges to sell. You could rent a stall at a market and wait for customers to come to you, or you could load all the fruit onto your bike and go find customers in the streets. Of course, those oranges would be a lot to carry, but if you were creative, you could do it. A car would be expensive, and it might not get you very far when streets were full of traffic.

In many countries, especially in Africa, bicycles serve as taxis. The first bicycle taxis in Kenya started off as a way to get across the border to Uganda without filling out paperwork. (Only people in motorized vehicles needed paperwork to cross.) To attract customers, the bicycle riders called out "border border," which sounded like "boda boda," and the bicycle taxis soon became known as *boda bodas*. People began using boda bodas not just to cross the border but also to get to places that were too far away to walk to. Now boda bodas are found all over Africa, and in many places they're people's favorite way of getting around.

On My Route

My friend Claudio loves baking bread. He loves cycling too. So when he decided to sell his bread at local farmers' markets, he bought a cargo tricycle and built a box for the front. The box stores everything he needs to sell his delicious creations at the market. He even built in a heater to keep his baking warm. Imagine riding a bike with the scent of freshly baked bread surrounding you!

Il Forno di Claudio (which means "the oven of Claudio") rolls into farmers' markets around Victoria each week. GASTÓN CASTAÑO

People around the world pedal their businesses through the streets, selling flowers, onions, bread—just about anything you can think of that might be sold from a bicycle. SITTHIVET SANTIKARN

Boda bodas transport people in lots of different situations. They bring students and teachers to school, businesspeople to work, the sick to the hospitals and even government ministers to important meetings. The passenger sits on the cushion on the back, and the taxi driver pedals. It's hot, difficult work. CYCLING OUT OF POVERTY—AFRICA

In India, bicycles are used to carry luggage. What a challenging ride that would be! HELEN COONEY

ALL PART OF THE JOB

Businesspeople aren't the only ones enjoying two-wheeled travel.

At Frederiksberg Hospital in Denmark, bicycles are important tools for nurses. Until a few years ago, elderly patients often needed to travel to the Emergency Department for simple treatments. These trips were stressful for patients and very expensive for the hospital. Now, whenever possible, nurses hop onto bicycles, zip through traffic jams to patients' homes and treat patients in comfort. Patients are happier, hospital bills are lower, and nurses have a chance to pedal around and enjoy the fresh air.

In Britain, mail carriers have delivered letters by bicycle since 1880. Gasoline is much more expensive in Europe than it is in

Pedal-powered vehicles don't always look the way we expect them to. This bicycle bus carries nine preschoolers through Amsterdam on field trips. WORKCYCLES/HENRY CUTLER

North America, so bicycles have saved the British postal service plenty of money. In 2010, though, the postal service decided to replace most of the bicycles with mail vans, out of concerns for safety and efficiency. This decision shocked people across the United Kingdom, especially because the government had just come up with a plan to get more people out riding bicycles!

MAKE WAY FOR BICYCLES

In Europe, many people use bicycles for short trips. In the Netherlands, cycling is so popular that about 30 to 40 percent of all trips are made by bicycle. Studies show that when more people ride bicycles, governments save money on road repair and health care. So in many countries the government ensures that pedaling is safe, easy and fun by creating plenty of bike paths and lots of bicycle parking.

BIKE FACTS: De Hoge Veluwe National Park in the Netherlands has seventeen hundred white bicycles for visitors to use while exploring the park. The bicycles are free to use, and no one is allowed to lock them up. Some days, all seventeen hundred bicycles are in use.

If you go to Bogotá, Colombia, this is a sign you'll see on the street. It says Bogotá—a bicycle-friendly place to ride on Sundays.
SARAH KAY HANSEN

Montreal, Quebec's Bixi bike-share program started in 2009. It now has more than 5,000 bicycles in 411 stations around the city.
PUBLIC BIKE SYSTEM COMPANY

Governments can promote cycling in other ways too. Bogotá, Colombia, hosted its first Ciclovia by closing off several major streets to cars. Now, every Sunday from 7:00 AM to 2:00 PM, as many as two million people flood the streets to walk or cycle together on over 100 kilometers (62 miles) of car-free streets. They stop for snacks at kiosks along the way, enjoy a concert or join an outdoor dance class at one of twenty stages set up for the day. People who participate say it's like having a citywide party every Sunday morning, all in celebration of people, community, bicycles, good health and fresh air. Bogotá has inspired cities around the world to start similar programs.

Another way to promote cycling is with a bike-share program. Many cities, such as Montreal and Toronto, have thousands of bicycles parked around the city for people to use. To borrow one, you pay a small fee to become a member of the program, and then each time you borrow a bicycle, you pay per hour and you can use the bike as long as you need it. When you're done with it, you lock it up in one of the program's many parking areas for someone else to use.

In countries where most adults have cars, many people still choose to ride a bicycle for work, errands and fun. Riding a bicycle helps solve the problems of pollution and obesity. In other countries, where people can't afford cars and often struggle to buy food, bicycles can help relieve poverty. How? Follow me and find out!

BIKE FACTS:
Planet Earth is home to approximately one billion bicycles. Nearly half of them are in China.

In Vietnam, bicycles can even be pet shops! This man is selling goldfish by the side of a road in Ho Chi Minh City.
ERIN PACKARD PHOTOGRAPHY/DREAMSTIME.COM

CHAPTER FOUR

Pedaling for Change

EMERGENCY!

What do you do if someone in your family has to go to the hospital? Chances are, you probably have a car, know someone with a car or could dial 9-1-1 for an ambulance.

But what if you live in a country that doesn't have a public ambulance system, you don't know anyone who has a car, and no one you know has enough money to pay for a taxi? How do you get to a hospital *then*?

In Namibia, cars are too expensive for most people. People get around mostly by walking, and until recently even health-care workers walked to their patients' homes. Many of their patients were so sick (often from HIV/AIDS or scorpion bites) that they needed to be in hospital, but the hospitals were too far away to get to without a car. Then an organization called the Bicycle Empowerment Network (BEN) gave bicycles to health-care workers to help them work more efficiently. BEN soon learned that healthcare workers also used them to do something that had been impossible before. If the hospital was only a few kilometers away, workers sat patients on the luggage rack of the bicycle and pedaled them to the nearest hospital.

This bicycle ambulance in Namibia allows people to get medical help far faster than they could before. AARON WHEELER

At your house, your stove probably runs on electricity or gas. In other parts of the world, though, most people cook over a fire made with wood or charcoal, which means someone has to bring the fuel home somehow. This man is bringing home wood in Malawi. JOACHIM LÖFFEL

In 2005, BEN started building bicycle ambulances. They've helped save many lives already, and they'll continue to save lives until all parts of Namibia have a public ambulance system.

PILE IT ON

In places where people can't afford cars, bicycles are the next-best option, for emergencies and for daily life. For many families, owning a bicycle saves hours every week because they can carry big loads of fuel for cooking fires or jugs of drinking water instead of making many trips. This means they can spend more time working to earn enough money for food. In many cultures, a bicycle is a prized possession because it helps families work more efficiently to put food and clean drinking water on the table.

Using a car to haul charcoal would make this Vietnamese girl's life much easier. Since her family can't afford a car, she uses a bicycle, which means she can haul far more than she could in a single walking trip. LON & QUETA

Bicycles can haul wide loads, too. This man in Vietnam is carrying sugar cane. STEPHEN BURES/DREAMSTIME.COM

In most countries, bicycles are an important way for adults to get around, but that doesn't stop these Vietnamese girls from trying them too. STEPHEN BURES/DREAMSTIME.COM

KID POWER!

Bicycles don't help just individual families. They can strengthen whole communities by helping young people get an education. Beene is a teenager in Zambia who could go to school only a few times a week until recently. The nearest school is eight kilometers (five miles) away, and she had to walk both ways, which took a lot of time. All that walking also made her legs hurt and left her too tired to concentrate. In 2011, though, an organization called World Bicycle Relief gave her a bicycle. Now she can get to school faster than before, and she still has enough energy to study, play sports after school, help look after her nieces and nephews and do other chores. She's going to school five days a week now, and she's well on her way to achieving her dream of becoming a nurse.

This bicycle in Malawi is saving its riders plenty of time as they run their errands. And errands are always more fun with company! KERRI FINLAYSON

In many countries, children live on the street because they've lost their families to war, hunger or disease, or their families can't afford to feed them. In the mid-1980s, Canadian Peter Dalglish was in war-torn Sudan. Every day he met children living on the street, and he realized they needed a way to earn money to buy food and a chance to go to school. He and a bunch of volunteers gathered several old bicycles, a few new T-shirts and the names of businesses that needed courier services,

The Street Kids International Bicycle Courier Service empowers kids to earn money to feed themselves and get an education. This photo was taken in Bangalore, India. STREET KIDS INTERNATIONAL'S STREET KIDS COURIERS

Between 1876 and 1907, people could buy this pedal-powered saw for ten dollars. The machine weighed 18 kg (40 lbs) and could cut up to 3.8 cm (1.5 in) of pine. GARY ROBERTS/ THE TOOLEMERA PRESS (WWW.TOOLEMERA.COM)

and together they started Street Kids International Bicycle Courier Service. Kids who once lived on the street now have legal, healthy and empowering ways to earn money, feed themselves and get an education. Street Kids International is today a worldwide organization that has worked with more than two million street kids in over sixty countries.

WHERE DID ALL THE PEDALS GO?

In places where people can't afford cars, a bicycle can make life much easier. But what if bicycles could do other things—like make electricity or power machines that usually use electricity?

It's not as crazy as it might sound. Back in the 1800s, almost as soon as the chain drive was invented, people began using pedal power to help them get their work done faster. Inventors attached chain drives and pedals to saws, grinders, shapers, tool sharpeners and drilling and cutting machines. In small workshops and households without electricity or steam power, pedal power made a world of difference in how much a person could do in a day.

As electricity became more common, people stopped using pedal power. But in many countries, electricity is still not available, or it's very expensive. About a quarter of the world's population does not have access to electricity. Kids do homework by lamp or firelight, and they don't use computers because there's nowhere to plug them in. Doctors in health clinics might have trouble helping patients because many medical tests need electricity. But pedal power can change all that.

AN ELECTRIFYING EXPERIENCE

Almost sixty percent of people in Nepal don't have electricity. But in the early 1990s, people in some parts of Nepal began making their own power with stationary bicycles. American engineer

In some places, people ride stationary bicycles to stay in shape. This man is pedaling to charge a battery that will help light his house at night. VILLAGETECH SOLUTIONS

David Sowerwine, a group of volunteers and a local builder had invented a pedal-powered electrical generator. With help from the World Bank, they set up generators in fourteen Nepalese villages. People came from miles around, hooked up small two-pound batteries to the bicycle system and pedaled to charge the batteries. Then they took their batteries home to power LEDs that gave two to three hours of light per night for up to two weeks. People also used the batteries to charge water sterilizers, cell phones and more.

Since solar power has become more available, these generators have been adapted to use the sun's energy so that no one has to pedal, but the bicycle generator was an important first step toward light for many villages.

BIKE FACTS: At a bicycle-powered movie theater in Vilnius, Lithuania, volunteer pedalers power the projector. When they get tired, they ring the bell, and another movie watcher takes over.

Bicimaquinas *are mostly for adults, but these children in San Andrés Itzapa, Guatemala, had fun pedaling to make smoothies. Adults can use pedal-powered blenders like this one to help make products to sell at the local market.* SAMUEL ABBOTT

In Afghanistan, kids in three cities are pedaling their way to an education—on pedal-powered laptops. An international organization called One Laptop Per Child (OLPC) has made twenty-five hundred pedal-powered laptops for kids to try out in schools. Electricity is available in these cities, but it's not always reliable. The laptops keep working even when the light switches don't.

BICIMAQUINAS

What's a *bicimaquina*? It means "bicycle machine" in Spanish, and since 2001 an organization called Maya Pedal has built more than two thousand of them. Maya Pedal receives bicycle donations from North America. Then mechanics and inventors attach the bicycles to other important machines. Local communities get together to buy a *bicimaquina* that everyone in the community can use. Today, instead of spending what little money they have on electricity, people can pedal to power water pumps, grinders, tool sharpeners, blenders and more.

LIFE-SAVING PEDAL POWER

What if a bicycle could help doctors treat a disability that affects over one billion people worldwide?

People with iron-deficiency anemia don't have enough healthy red blood cells. Doctors can find out if a patient has this problem by putting a blood sample in a machine called a centrifuge. The centrifuge spins the sample around so fast that the blood separates into a liquid part and a more solid part. The solid part is the red blood cells. By comparing the two parts, an experienced healthcare worker can see if the patient has iron-deficiency anemia.

But what if there's no electricity to make the centrifuge work? And what if it breaks and the replacement parts are too expensive or unavailable? In India, where iron-deficiency anemia is especially common, healthcare workers often face these problems with centrifuges.

A team of university students in the United States has invented the CentriCycle—a centrifuge that doesn't need electricity or expensive parts. CentriCycles are built out of bicycle parts, and healthcare workers power them by hand. The CentriCycle team hopes that someday soon their centrifuges will be helping people all over India.

In CentriCycle's centrifuge, blood-sample tubes fit into holders between the spokes. The healthcare worker spins the pedal for eight minutes and analyzes the results. No electricity needed!
CENTRICYCLE/SARAH SCHWENDEMAN

BIKE FACTS: Several health clubs in North America have hooked up their stationary bikes so that the people working out on them actually help power the building.

PEDALING TOGETHER

Around the world, people are using similar bicycles to relieve very different kinds of problems, from pollution and obesity in some countries to poverty in others. But one thing most bicycle owners have in common is how much they love their two-wheeled vehicles. And as time goes by, people are loving them even more.

When cars were invented, no one knew that the fuel would cause problems for the environment. In the same way, when people first started using electricity, no one was concerned about conserving power. Now that we know more about these valuable resources, though, people are making different choices. Choosing appropriate technology for each situation can both protect the environment and keep us fit.

If anyone's ever given you a bicycle, you've got something in common with the millions of people around the world who depend on them every day. A bicycle is much more than a fun way to get around. It's a life-changing tool that can really take you places!

On My Route

In Buenos Aires, Argentina, I heard a strange whistle and the rattle of an old bicycle on bumpy pavement. I soon learned that knife sharpeners across the country use a whistle with the same combination of notes to call out to people who need their knives sharpened. When a customer appears, the cyclist props the bike on a kickstand that raises the rear wheel off the ground. Then he climbs on and pedals to turn the sharpening stone. His setup is cheap, and the only power he needs comes from his legs. Brilliant!

The pedal-powered knife sharpener that inspired this book. MICHELLE MULDER

This Buddhist monk in Laos is one of millions of people who love their bicycles.
DIGITALPRESS/DREAMSTIME.COM

Resources

Books

Haduch, Bill. *Go Fly a Bike! The Ultimate Book About Bicycle Fun, Freedom & Science.* New York, NY: Dutton Children's Books, 2004.

Macy, Sue. *Wheels of Change: How Women Rode the Bicycle to Freedom (With a Few Flat Tires Along the Way).* Washington, DC: National Geographic Society, 2011.

Movies

Ciclovia: http://www.streetfilms.org/ciclovia/

Websites

Bamboo Bike Project: http://bamboobike.org/

Bicycle Empowerment Network of Namibia: http://benbikes.org.za/namibia/

Bicycles for Humanity: http://www.bicycles-for-humanity.org/

CentriCycle: http://www.centricycle.com/

The Exploratorium's Science of Cycling: Bicycle Physics and History: http://www.exploratorium.edu/cycling/

The Human-Powered Home: Choosing Muscle Over Motors: http://www.thehumanpoweredhome.com/links

Maya Pedal: http://www.mayapedal.org/

Streetkids International: http://www.streetkids.org/

World Bicycle Relief: http://www.worldbicyclerelief.org/

Acknowledgments

It takes a village to raise a child, and it took a global village to write this book. *Pedal It!* exists because of the passion and generosity of cycling enthusiasts around the world who answered emails from this random Canadian children's author. People from Afghanistan to Zambia sent me photos, tips, contacts and encouragement, and I'd like to say a big thank-you to each of them, so hold onto your handlebars. Here goes…

Thanks to the dear cycling friends who gathered in my living room to bounce around ideas for this book: Tim Judge, Bob McInnes and Mark Weston. You and your love of cycling are an inspiration. I'm grateful to Kari Jones, who mentioned the term "appropriate technology" and instantly clarified what I was trying to say. Thanks also to Drew at Tall Tales Books, who helped with market research. Long live independent bookstores!

I'm grateful to Simon Wigzell and Felicity Perrman of the Greater Victoria Cycling Coalition, as well as Michael Coo at Tour d'Afrique, for their enthusiasm and help in finding photos. For the spectacular images, contacts and information from around the world, I send heartfelt thanks to Ian Paul, Emillie Parrish, Emily Boyle, Margriet Ruurs, Andreas Lutz, J.D. Gibbard, Marilyn Kan, Lorne Shields, Helen Cooney, Joachim Löffel, Kerri Finlayson, Lon Brehmer and Enriqueta Flores-Guevara, Zach Vanderkooy, Henry Cutler, Avi Silberstein, Chris Wille, Michael Linke, David Sowerine, Sitthivet Santikarn, John Mutter, Luuk Eickmans, Sarah Kay Hansen, Carolyn Yarina, Gary Roberts, Mila Czemerys, James Schwartz, Betty and Bob McInnes, Susan Braley, Aaron Wheeler, Martin Kuenzler, Lucas Torresi, Sarah Schwendeman, The Public Bike

System Company, Street Kids International, City of Münster Press Office and the nice fellow at NASA who answered my strange questions about bicycle-powered flight. Bill Haduch's book *Go Fly a Bike! The Ultimate Book About Bicycle Fun, Freedom & Science* was an enormous help in my understanding of the scientific principles that keep a bike upright. I'm also grateful to Florence Feldman-Wood, Peter Teal and Kris De Decker, who offered expert opinions on an obscure idea. Thanks, too, to Kathleen Wilker at *Momentum Mag* for spreading the word about this book project.

When I couldn't find the photos I needed, many people generously stepped in to help. Thank you to the kids who agreed to be photographed for the book: Maia, Luke, Paige, Oliver and Orin. Thanks also to Colby, Claudio, Gregorio and Kimberly and her family for allowing me to include their photos. An extra-special thank-you goes to Sarah Claudette and Samuel Abbott, who arranged a photo shoot in Guatemala especially for this project.

I am grateful to Orca Book Publishers for taking a chance on my first nonfiction book. Many thanks to Sarah Harvey for her guidance and insightful editing, and to Teresa Bubela for her beautiful book design.

I especially want to thank my husband, Gastón Castaño, for his encouragement and intrepid wielding of the camera at a moment's notice. And thanks to all my friends, too, for listening to me talk and talk and talk about how excited I am about bicycles and this book!

Thank you, everyone.

Index

Index (continued)